Weather

Barnes & Noble Publishing, Inc.
122 Fifth Avenue
New York, NY 10011

ISBN 0-7607-4639-7

Printed and bound in China

06 07 08 09 MCH 10 9 8 7 6

Color reproduction by Colourscan Co Pte Ltd

DISCOVERIES

Weather

CONSULTING EDITOR

David Ellyard
Weather Consultant

BARNES & NOBLE

NEW YORK

Contents

• WEATHER FORECASTING •

• CLIMATE •

• CLIMATIC CHANGE •

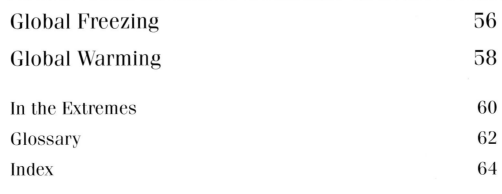

What is Weather?

The weather affects all things on Earth. It helps to shape our landscapes and provide our food supplies. The weather influences the way we live, where we live, what we wear, the running of transportation systems and even how we feel. Extreme weather can bring storms that destroy homes, or droughts that can ruin crops. But what exactly is weather? It is the conditions that exist in the air around us at any one time: the temperature and pressure of the atmosphere, the amount of moisture it holds, and the presence or absence of wind and clouds. The weather is very hard to predict, and it can be incredibly diverse locally. One side of a mountain, for example, may be buffeted by high winds, while the other side may have no wind at all.

BURNING UP
Intense summer heat may help to ignite trees and cause dramatic fires. If these fires are fanned by high winds, they can move quickly through brushland.

BLOWN AWAY
Some of the strongest winds are associated with hurricanes. These huge tropical storms bring heavy rain and high winds.

SNOW FALLS
In cold weather, heavy falls of snow can make it difficult to move around.

FOOD PRODUCTION

Rain is very important to the production of food. When there is plenty of rain, crops grow and give good yields, and animals have plenty of water. But if it does not rain, even for just a few weeks, the effects can be disastrous. The soil can become parched and crops may wither and die. If this happens, grazing animals do not have enough food to eat and water supplies start to stagnate.

UNDER THE SUN
Vast areas become parched and dry when it does not rain for months on end.

RAINBOW
A mixture of sunlight and rain often creates this colorful sight in the sky.

FLOOD
Storm clouds bring heavy rain. Rivers can burst their banks and flood low-lying land, washing away buildings and crops.

Discover more in Global Warming

The Weather Engine

The sun fuels the world's weather. The surface of the Earth is warmed by sunlight. The tropics are heated most intensely, while the two poles receive the least heat. Only half the energy coming from the sun to the Earth is absorbed by the Earth's surface. The other half is reflected back into space or absorbed into the atmosphere. Different surfaces reflect varying amounts of heat. Bright white snow can reflect 90 percent of the sun's energy, so very little heat remains. The dark green tropical rainforests, however, absorb a large amount of energy. Temperatures on land change more than those in the oceans. These differences generate pressure patterns that cause winds to blow. They also set in motion the vast circulation of the atmosphere, which produces the world's weather and climate.

HEAT FROM THE SUN
Because the Earth is a sphere, air is warmed more at the equator than at the poles. Rays of sunlight contain certain amounts of energy. Depending on the season, rays will fall on small circular areas near the equator. At the poles, however, the rays are spread over a wider area because they hit the Earth at an angle. If the heat at the equator was not distributed by wind and water, the equator would get hotter and hotter.

DID YOU KNOW?
The amount of solar energy that reaches the Earth's atmosphere every 24 hours is similar to the amount of energy that would be released by 200 million electric power stations during the same period of time.

Wind

The air around us is always on the move. It creates both gentle breezes and wild gale-force winds. Air begins to move when the sun heats the land and warms the air above. Molecules in the air move faster when they are heated and the air starts to expand. It becomes less dense than the surrounding air, and creates an area of low pressure. Like a huge, invisible bubble, the warm air rises through the surrounding cooler air. At the same time, cooler, heavier air is drawn in below to replace the rising air. This circulation of air is called a convection current. The speed at which wind moves is determined by air pressure. Wind blows from areas of high pressure to areas of low pressure. Low pressure systems are therefore associated with unsettled and windy weather while high pressure systems bring fine and calm weather.

RAIN SHADOW
Most mountains experience a warm, dry wind, which blows down the sheltered side. Moisture is deposited on the windward side.

Going down
Air sinks over cool areas, such as the sea.

DAY BREEZES
On warm, sunny days, sea breezes blow on the coast. These onshore breezes are caused by differences in temperature between the hot land and cool water. At night, however, the temperature of the land falls rapidly below that of the sea. The breeze changes direction and blows offshore.

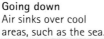

VALLEY WIND
As mountain slopes are heated by the sun, the warm air rises. This cools and falls, creating a cool wind as it fills the space left by the rising warm air.

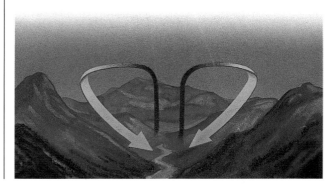

MOUNTAIN WIND
At night, warm mountain air cools and flows down the mountain slopes into the valley, creating a cool wind.

From the sea
Wind blows from the sea as cool air flows toward the city to replace the rising warm air.

Wild Winds

A hot, humid spring day on the central plains of North America can spell danger. These conditions are perfect for the formation of tornadoes, or "twisters." These violent and unpredictable whirlwinds are the strongest winds on Earth. A tornado is only between 33 ft (10 m) and 1,300 ft (400 m) across, but it is accompanied by heavy rain, thunder and lightning. It is extremely powerful and destructive. Hurricanes are giant wind storms, more than 250 miles (400 km) in diameter. The largest can spread more than 1,240 miles (2,000 km). They can last for many hours bringing torrential rain and strong winds. Less than 100 hurricanes occur each year and most never come near land. But the few that do cross onto land can create havoc as crops, forests—even complete towns—are ruthlessly destroyed. These giant storms occur around the world under different names: they are hurricanes in the Atlantic and eastern Pacific oceans, cyclones in the Pacific and Indian oceans, and typhoons in the northwest Pacific.

WATERSPOUTS
These winds form between sea and cloud. The wind draws water up from the sea to form a whirling column of water and spray.

The beginning
Wild winds develop deep within thunderclouds when warm, moist air meets cool, dry air moving in the opposite direction, and is forced to rise.

Spinning out
Winds within the thunderclouds cause the warm air to spin. The column of warm air spins faster and faster.

On the move
A funnel of spinning air projects down through the cloud base toward the ground. Once formed, a tornado can move across the ground at speeds of up to 60 miles (100 km) per hour.

PATH OF DESTRUCTION
The funnel of a tornado is like a vacuum cleaner, sucking up everything in its path. Within the funnel-shaped cloud, the wind may reach speeds of more than 186 miles (300 km) per hour. Tornadoes rarely last for more than half an hour, but they are tremendously strong. Buildings and trees in the direct path of a tornado are often destroyed, but those just a few yards either side may survive.

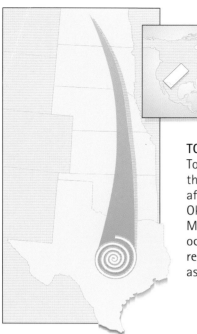

TORNADO ALLEY
Tornadoes occur all over the world, but the worst affected areas are Kansas, Oklahoma and Missouri. More than 700 tornadoes occur here each year. The region is sometimes known as "tornado alley."

ODD MISSILES
Objects thrown great distances at high speed can turn into dangerous missiles. At more than 186 miles (300 km) per hour, even a piece of straw can kill.

THE ATMOSPHERE

The atmosphere is an envelope of air that surrounds the Earth. It extends to a height of 434 miles (700 km), but there is no clear boundary as to where it ends and space begins. The atmosphere has four layers. The lowest layer is the troposphere where the air contains lots of water vapor and dust. Most of the world's weather occurs in this layer. The stratosphere has dry, warm air and this is where the ozone layer is found. The mesosphere is a colder layer and temperatures can fall to -184°F (-120°C). The thermosphere is the outer layer and the gases here are very thin. As the gases absorb ultraviolet light, the temperatures climb to as high as 3632°F (2000°C). Auroras and meteors are seen in this layer.

Thermosphere
above 50 miles (80 km)

Mesosphere
30–50 miles (50–80 km)

Stratosphere
6–30 miles (10–50 km)

Troposphere
0–6 miles (0–10 km)

MOVING WATER
The world's oceans greatly affect weather and climate. Water evaporates, which causes clouds and rain, and currents move heat from the equator to the poles.

UPS AND DOWNS
The shape of the Earth influences the weather. Mountains can deflect the wind and rain. The Himalayan mountain system has a major effect on the summer monsoon in Asia.

KEEPING CONTROL
The polar ice caps act as thermostats for the world's weather and climate. The ice and snow reflect much of the sun's energy, and any change in the area of the ice caps can affect global temperatures.

Discover more in Winds and Currents

Hot and sticky
This hygrometer shows a 90 percent humidity reading.

Temperature and Humidity

If you were standing in the Sahara Desert, the air would feel hot and dry. If you were lying on a tropical beach, it would feel hotter, even though the temperature may be the same in both places. The reason for this difference is humidity—the amount of moisture or water vapor in the air. Humans can only tolerate a certain range of temperature and humidity. Sweating helps to keep the body cool. But if the air is very humid, water does not evaporate so easily and sweat remains on the skin. This can be uncomfortable and makes you feel hotter. Humidity is measured with an instrument called a hygrometer. A simple hygrometer uses two thermometers: one has a bulb that is surrounded by a wet cloth, while the other is dry. If the air is very dry, the "wet bulb" is cooled rapidly by evaporation. But if the air is very humid, little evaporation occurs and the reading of the two thermometers is almost the same.

GROWING CONDITIONS
A desert and a rainforest often have similar air temperatures, but lush vegetation can only grow in the rainforest because the air is very moist, or humid. The heat of the desert, however, is very dry. This lack of moisture means that few plants can survive.

KEEPING COOL
In hot weather, or when we exercise, our body temperature may rise above 98.6°F (37°C). Special glands on the surface of the skin release sweat. The evaporation of this watery fluid cools our bodies.

HURRICANES

Hurricanes start life as small thunderstorms over warm water. The warm water heats the air above it and creates a rising current of warm, moist air. Cooler air is pulled in to replace the rising current. Huge banks of cumulonimbus clouds build up. Several storms may group together, as winds within the clouds begin to blow. The whole storm spins as it moves forward. As the hurricane rotates, it draws in warm moist air from the ocean, gaining energy all the time.

EYE OF THE STORM
At the center of a hurricane, surrounded by a huge wall of clouds, is a small calm area called the "eye of the storm." The air rises and spins in the clouds, but in the eye, the air sinks. As the eye of the storm passes overhead, the rain stops and there is a brief period of calm before the second part of the storm arrives.

13

HURRICANE DAMAGE
Hurricane-force winds and heavy rain can devastate an area. Coastal regions may be flooded by the storm surge that follows the winds. Only the strongest buildings will survive.

FROM SPACE
Satellites are used to track the course of hurricanes so that early warning can be given to regions in the path of the storm.

FORCES OF WIND

In 1805, Sir Francis Beaufort, an English admiral, devised a scale to measure the force of wind by observing changes in the waves and the effects of different winds on the sails of British warships. Later, his scale was adapted for use on land. The Beaufort scale, which is still used by meteorologists, ranges from 0 (calm) to force 12 (strong winds associated with hurricanes).

Force	Speed (per hour)		Description	Effect
	miles	km		
0	1	1	calm	smoke moves straight up
1	3	5	light air	smoke slightly bent
2	7	11	light breeze	leaves rustle
3	11	18	gentle breeze	leaves move
4	19	30	moderate breeze	small branches move
5	24	39	fresh breeze	small trees sway
6	31	50	strong breeze	large branches move
7	38	61	moderate gale	whole trees sway
8	46	74	fresh gale	twigs break off
9	54	87	strong gale	roofs damaged
10	63	102	gale	trees uprooted
11	73	117	storm	widespread damage
12	74+	120+	hurricane	widespread destruction

On the move
Warm air spreads out at high altitudes.

Moving up
The air over the land, particularly city areas, warms during the day. This warm air rises into the atmosphere.

MEASURING THE TEMPERATURE

Anders Celsius

In 1714, the German scientist Gabriel Fahrenheit invented the temperature scale. The zero point was based on the lowest point to which the mercury fell during the winter in Germany. The freezing point of water was 32°F, while the boiling point was 212°F. In 1742, the Swedish astronomer Anders Celsius proposed an alternative scale. He suggested making the freezing point of water 0°C and the boiling point of water 100°C. This scale was very useful for scientific work, and it is used more widely than Fahrenheit's scale.

Hot and dry
This hygrometer shows a humidity reading of 20 percent.

A FROZEN DESERT
Antarctica is the coldest place on Earth. Its freezing air tends to be extremely dry because very cold air holds only a small amount of water vapor.

Fronts
When masses of air of different temperatures meet, the warm air is forced to rise. Clouds appear as the warm air rises and this is called a warm front.

CLOUD FORMATION
Clouds can form in many ways but they all involve warm moist air coming into contact with cooler air.

Current collision
When currents of air collide, they force each other upward.

• THE DAILY WEATHER •

What are Clouds?

Clouds are masses of water droplets and ice crystals that float in the sky. They are formed by a process that begins when warm moist air rises. As the warm air cools, it is unable to hold water vapor. Some of the water vapor condenses around dust particles and forms minute water droplets. These tiny drops make up clouds. The sky can be covered with a blanket of cloud that is formed when a mass of warm air rises above cooler air and causes the water vapor to condense. Clouds also form when warm air is forced to rise over mountains, or when warm air blows over a colder surface such as cool water. On hot days, storm clouds appear when warm moist air rises and then cools rapidly. Clouds appear to be white because the water droplets reflect light. As a cloud becomes thicker and heavier with droplets, it darkens because light cannot pass through it.

AN AERIAL VIEW
Seen from above, the tops of clouds often look like a white blanket or a field of snow.

18

Water droplets
Millions of microscopic droplets of water are needed to make one drop of rain.

THE WATER CYCLE

Water covers more than 70 percent of the Earth's surface. Warmth from the sun causes some of the water to evaporate from the surface of oceans, lakes and rivers, as well as from plants. This water vapor rises and cools, and then condenses back into water to form clouds. The water droplets fall as rain or snow, which runs into rivers and lakes and can sometimes soak into underground layers of rock. Eventually, the water returns to the oceans to complete the cycle.

Convection
On a sunny day, some patches of ground warm up more quickly than others. Bubbles of warm air form over these spots and rise into the sky. As the bubbles rise, they expand and cool. The water condenses and forms a cumulus cloud that is shaped like a dome.

In the clouds
When warm air meets a mountain range, it is forced upward. The warm air cools and banks of clouds form around the mountain peaks.

CLOUD BANK
Banks of clouds are often seen lying over mountain ranges.

Cirrus

32,800 ft (10,000 m)

Cirrocumulus

Cirrostratus

19,700 ft (6,000 m)

HIGH IN THE SKY
The three main cloud groups are based on height. High clouds are more than 19,700 ft (6,000 m); middle clouds are 6,600–19,700 ft (2,000–6,000 m); and low clouds are under 6,600 ft (2,000 m). Cumulonimbus clouds tower higher than 32,800 ft (10,000 m).

Altocumulus

Altostratus

Cumulonimbus

6,600 ft (2,000 m)

Stratocumulus

Stratus

Cumulus

Nimbostratus

Types of Cloud

No two clouds are exactly the same. Although they vary in shape and size, they can be divided broadly into two similar types: heaped, fluffy clouds; and layered clouds. Heaped clouds are formed when pockets of warm air drift upward, while layered clouds are created by moist air moving horizontally between cooler layers. Clouds are usually grouped according to how high they are above the ground. It is important to identify different types of cloud because they give us information about the weather. White, puffy cumulus clouds, for example, are associated with warm sunny days. High cirrus clouds mark the approach of a weather front (an advancing mass of warm or cold air). Cirrus clouds may be followed by lower altostratus clouds and low stratus rain clouds, which cover the entire sky in a solid gray sheet.

BUBBLING SKIES
These pendulous clouds, called mammatus clouds, form below the anvil of a thundercloud. They are frequently seen with storms that produce tornadoes.

FLYING SAUCERS
These lenticular, or lens-shaped, clouds have been mistaken for flying saucers. They usually form in bands on the sheltered side of mountain ranges.

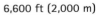

MIXED SKIES

At least five cloud types are visible in this busy sky. In the background, a huge pale cumulonimbus thundercloud fills the sky. Along the lower edge, dark rain-bearing stratus clouds underlie paler, fluffier cumulus clouds. The strong, dark streaks at the middle level are altostratus, with altocumulus above and below.

DID YOU KNOW?

Cumulonimbus are the largest clouds and can tower 11 miles (18 km) into the sky. These clouds may contain up to 110,000 tons (100,000 tonnes) of water.

VAPOR TRAILS

Some aircraft leave white vapor trails as they fly across a clear blue sky. These "artificial clouds" are caused when the hot exhaust gases from the jet engines mix with the surrounding cold air and cool rapidly. Water vapor within the exhaust freezes and forms a trail of ice crystals.

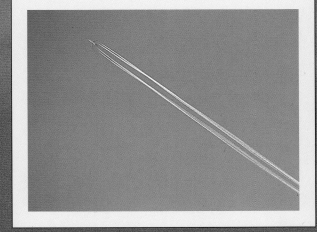

Thunder and Lightning

O n a hot, humid summer day, strong rising convection currents of warm air form cumulus clouds that soon grow into a towering cumulonimbus cloud, or thundercloud. These black clouds are accompanied by strong winds, heavy rain, lightning and thunder, and often produce spectacular summer storms. Most lightning occurs in cumulonimbus clouds because they contain violent currents of air and a plentiful supply of super-cooled droplets of water. The intense heating of the air by lightning causes the air to expand at supersonic speed and produces a clap of thunder. Lightning and thunder occur at the same time, but as light travels faster than sound, we see the flash before we hear the thunder. We can tell how far away a storm is by timing the interval between the flash and the thunder. A three-second interval represents a distance of $^{6}/_{10}$ mile (1 km).

LIGHTNING STRIKE
Lightning usually strikes the highest point, such as a tall building or an isolated tree, so it is dangerous to shelter beneath a tree during a thunderstorm. You would be much safer in a car.

RIBBON LIGHTNING
Strong winds may cause lightning to move and give a ribbonlike effect.

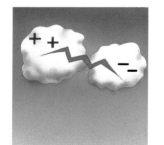

CLOUD TO GROUND
Lightning can form when there is a build up of negative charges at the bottom of a cloud and the ground below is positively charged.

CLOUD TO CLOUD
Lightning may occur between a negatively charged cloud and a nearby cloud that is positively charged.

INSIDE A CLOUD
Most lightning forms within a cloud, when there is a discharge between a positive and negative charge.

DID YOU KNOW?
Lightning strikes the Earth as frequently as 100 times every second. These strikes are produced by the 2,000 thunderstorms that rage around the world at any one moment in time.

BALLS OF FIRE
Sometimes, lightning appears as a fiery ball. Some balls disappear quietly, while others explode. Some have even appeared to chase people! Fortunately, ball lightning is very unusual and seldom causes harm.

LIFE OF A THUNDERCLOUD

Strong currents build up within a developing thundercloud. These turbulent currents cause ice crystals within the cloud to continually rise and fall. The ice crystals become heavier and heavier as fresh layers of ice are added to the crystals. Toward the end of the thundercloud's life, the ice crystals are so heavy that the air currents cannot keep them airborne. Instead, they fall to the ground as ice and rain. This marks the end of the thunderstorm and the cloud begins to break up.

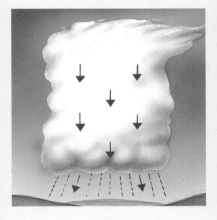

A dying thunderstorm

Rain, Hail and Snow

The water or ice that falls from a cloud is called precipitation. This may be in the form of rain, drizzle, sleet, snow or hail. The conditions within a cloud, and the temperature outside it, determine the type of precipitation that falls. One important factor is whether the cloud is high enough above the ground for the water droplets in it to turn into ice. The height at which this occurs is called the freezing level. It can be as little as 1,000 ft (300 m) or as high as 16,000 ft (5,000 m) above the ground. Snow falls from low and very cold clouds when the air temperature is around freezing, so the ice crystals can reach the ground without melting. If snow falls into air that is just above freezing, some of the crystals melt and produce a mixture of rain and snow called sleet. Dark cumulonimbus clouds bring thunderstorms, which may be accompanied by hail. A blanket of thin nimbostratus clouds produces a steady stream of rain, while low stratus clouds bring drizzle.

RAINY DAYS
A low blanket of gray clouds often brings a steady downpour that can last for an hour or more. However, drizzle and light rain can last for much longer.

Rain
Rain forms when tiny water droplets collect around small ice crystals until they become heavy enough to fall.

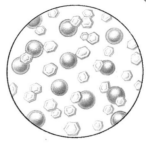

Upper layer
The temperature here can be as low as -32°F (-40°C) and the clouds, which are spread out, are formed mainly of ice crystals.

Middle layer
Strong air currents carry ice crystals and water droplets high into the atmosphere.

Lower layer
This lower layer is close to freezing. Water vapor comes up from the ground and condenses to form a cloud.

Hail
Hail forms around small ice crystals. As strong air currents circulate repeatedly and cause layers of ice to build up around the crystals, hailstones become larger.

Snow
Snow forms if the freezing level is below a height of 1,000 ft (300 m) above the ground, and the ice crystals do not have time to melt before they reach the ground.

STRANGE BUT TRUE
In 1953, hailstones as large as golf balls fell in Alberta, Canada. They covered an area 140 miles (225 km) by 5 miles (8 km) and killed thousands of birds.

HAIL STORM
Hail can cause great damage everywhere. This crop was ruined completely by these large hailstones.

THE SHAPE OF A SNOWFLAKE
Snowflakes are loose clusters of ice crystals usually with a flat, six-sided (hexagonal) shape. The exact shape of a snowflake depends on the temperature of the air, and no two snowflakes are the same. At very low temperatures, small needlelike crystals form, while at temperatures nearer to freezing, larger branching shapes are more common. The amount of water vapor in the air is important: at lower temperatures there is less water vapor and the crystals that form tend to be smaller.

Discover more in What are Clouds?

Fog, Frost and Ice

Clear nights with low ground temperatures often bring fog and frost, especially around dawn. The clear skies allow heat to radiate into space, and the temperature drops toward freezing. Moisture in the air condenses near the ground to form low-lying fog or mist. In the morning, the sun heats the air and the fog disperses. If the temperature is low enough, moisture in the air freezes and coats the ground, plants and other surfaces with a thin layer of frozen dew or frost. In long periods of cold, the surfaces of ponds and lakes freeze over, while dripping water freezes into icicles. Smog is a visible form of air pollution that often occurs in cities. It can be caused by the smoke from cars and huge industrial chimneys. Smog can affect everyone, but especially the health of the young, the old and those with lung problems.

COLD AND FROSTY MORNINGS

On clear nights, heat from the ground escapes back into space. Temperatures near the ground may be low enough for ice to form. Hoar frost is a coating of tiny ice crystals. If there is an icy wind, the temperature drops further and a thick coating of ice appears on exposed surfaces. This is called rime frost.

ICY FEATHERS

On winter mornings, windows are sometimes covered with beautiful patterns of ice crystals. This happens when moisture comes into contact with the cold window and is cooled to the freezing point.

TYPES OF FOG

Different conditions form different types of fog. An advection fog is produced when warm, moist air blows over a cooler surface. Radiation, or ground, fog occurs on clear nights, especially in river valleys where the ground cools quickly and moisture in the air condenses. Upslope fog is created when air is forced to rise up the side of a hill and cools, which causes moisture in the air to condense. Frontal fogs form when weather fronts, especially warm fronts, pass through a cooler area.

A WALL OF ICE
Sometimes it is so cold that ocean spray freezes, and a wall of ice forms along the shoreline.

DID YOU KNOW?

Before the invention of refrigerators, ice was cut from ponds in winter and stored in an ice house. The ice house was a pit, packed with layers of ice and straw and covered with an insulated roof. Cold air sinks, so the pit remained very cold and the ice lasted right through the summer.

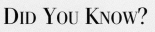

GHOSTLY SHADOWS
Sometimes, the sun projects enlarged shadows of mountain climbers onto low-lying clouds. This creates a ghostly effect called a Brocken Specter.

ROLLING ALONG
Snow rollers are created when the wind lifts a thin layer of snow from a lake or field to create a cylindrical shape.

COLOR OF LIGHT
Sunlight is called white light, but it is really a mixture of different colors. Rays of sunlight are bent as they pass into the raindrop. They reflect off the back of the drop and bend again as they leave.

• THE DAILY WEATHER •
Weather Wonders

You can often see strange effects in the sky. When sunlight hits ice crystals or water droplets, some of the colors of light are reflected. This creates phenomena such as rainbows, sundogs and glories. The multicolored arc of a rainbow stretching across the sky directly opposite the sun is one of the most colorful sights in the sky. Rainbows occur during isolated showers or thunderstorms, when falling rain is illuminated by sunlight. Sundogs, or parhelia, are small suns that appear on either side of the sun. They are created when ice crystals bend light in high clouds. When water droplets in the clouds reflect sunlight back toward the sun, alternating red and blue rings—called glories—are visible beneath the sun. Colored rain is an unusual weather wonder. Red sand carried from desert areas by the wind can cause red rain, while soot in the air can result in black rain. Yellow rain, caused by pollen, is very rare.

SUNDOGS
These are images that appear to the left and right of the sun at the same height above the horizon. They are called sundogs because they often have long, white tails that point away from the sun.

SEEING DOUBLE

Rainbows are caused by the reflection of sunlight in millions of raindrops. The sun must be behind you and fairly low for a rainbow to be visible in the sky. This is why rainbows are never seen in the middle of the day. Sometimes, if the light has been reflected twice inside each raindrop, a second fainter rainbow can be seen about 9 degrees outside the first. The colors are reversed in order, with red on the inside.

51° 42°

FALLING FROM THE SKY

An old saying, "it's raining cats and dogs," may not be as strange as it sounds. Strong storm winds can suck up quite large objects. In October 1968, during a heavy storm in Acapulco, Mexico, maggots reportedly rained down on boats in the harbor. Stories of fish and frogs falling from the sky have been told around the world for centuries. The record books also tell of worms, snails and even snakes raining on surprised people.

Natural Clues

Long before people came to rely on weather forecasts, they looked to nature for signs that would tell them about the weather. Knowledge of the weather is important because people need to know what clothes to wear, what plants to grow, and when to harvest their crops. The livelihoods of farmers and fishermen still depend on knowing what the weather might do in the future. Farmers from the past observed the color of the sky and the way in which the behavior of animals changed with the weather patterns. Not all signs were reliable, for many were based on superstition, but some were accurate enough to help them plan ahead. This kind of weather forecasting is thousands of years old and dates back as far as the ancient Greeks. Often, information about the weather was in the form of rhymes and songs that could be passed down from generation to generation.

A NOD OF THE HEAD
When a donkey sways and nods its head, the Spanish believe that rain will soon fall from the skies.

FLYING LOW
Some people in Asia believe that rain is on the way when dragonflies hover just above the ground.

CLEAN CATS
In Germany, some believe that a cat washes itself just before a shower of rain.

FOWL WEATHER
When African guinea fowl begin to pair off and build a nest, it is a sign that rain is due to fall.

RED SKY AT NIGHT

In many parts of the world, people believe that a red sky at night indicates fine weather while a red sky in the morning means bad weather is on the way. As the red color of the sky is created only when the clouds above reflect the light of the setting sun, this is accurate only when clouds come in from the west!

BUZZING AROUND

Bees in flight, busy collecting food, are said to be a sign of fine weather.

A GLORIOUS DAY

If the flowers of the morning-glory are open, some weather watchers predict fine weather.

THE TRUTH IN THE TALE

Many natural weather clues have no scientific basis whatsoever, but there are some that prove to be surprisingly accurate. A "ring around the moon" is a fair indicator that it will rain within the next few days. The ring is actually a watery halo made up from ice crystals in cirrostratus clouds. A red sky at night is frequently followed by a fine day. African guinea fowl are able to hear the rumble of thunder hundreds of miles away, so their nesting behavior is a reliable forecast of rain. Flowers, grasshoppers and bees, however, are generally poor predictors of changes in the weather.

ALL DRIED OUT

Some people believe that if they find pine cones with their scales open, the weather will remain fine and dry.

WARMING UP

Grasshoppers tend to chirp during warm, dry weather. As the temperature increases, their chirping becomes louder and louder.

Discover more in Types of Cloud

Weather Myths

People have always been intrigued by the mysteries of the weather. Long before weather forecasting became a science, people tried to explain the weather by creating stories about the sun, wind and rain. They invented gods to represent the elements and myths for frightening events such as thunder and lightning. The powerful Norse god Thor, for example, was said to carry a hammer. Every time he used it in anger, thunder and lightning would strike. Some people in Asia believed that typhoons sweeping across the China Sea were caused by a monstrous bird flapping its wings. When there were droughts, people often called upon their gods to send rain. The Hopi Indians in North America performed a snake dance because they believed it would bring rain. Hopi snake priests danced around the village square with live rattlesnakes, which represented the lightning of the summer rains, in their mouths. Some cultures even made sacrifices to their gods. The Aztecs offered their children to the rain god Tlaloc to make sure there was always plenty of rain.

STOPPING THE THUNDER
In Nigeria, the Yoruba priests have special ceremonies where they hold up a staff carved with the image of their god of thunder and lightning. This is supposed to ward off thunderstorms.

THUNDERBIRDS
Some Native Americans believe that giant birds called Thunderbirds beat their wings to produce thunder. The flashing of their eyes creates lightning.

32

CHINESE STORM GODS

An ancient Chinese myth tells how a thunderstorm is created by different gods. Lei Kung, the Thunder God, is helped by Tien Mu, Mother Lightning. She produces lightning using mirrors in her hands. Yu-tzu, the Master of the Rain, sprinkles water from his pot with a sword. The Little Boy of the Clouds, Yun-tíung, piles up the clouds, while the Earl of the Wind, Feng-po, releases blustery winds from a goatskin bag.

STORM SPIRIT

Kultana is an Aboriginal spirit from Arnhem Land, Australia. It is linked to the north wind and rain.

DID YOU KNOW?

In the past, people from many cultures interpreted the weather as signs from the gods. Angry gods might send lightning to strike a person or place.

SUN WORSHIP

The sun is important in our lives—it brings heat and light and ripens crops. Many cultures worshipped this powerful source of energy. In South America, the Inca and Aztec civilizations built temples and shrines to the sun god. The Temple of the Sun at Teotihuacán in Mexico is shaped like a pyramid. A small dwelling for the god at the top of the temple is reached by a huge staircase. Many of the temples were positioned so that observers could watch the sun's passage at the summer solstice (the longest day of the year).

History of Forecasting

In the seventeenth century, the Accademia del Cimento (Academy of Experiments) in Florence, Italy, was the center for scientific investigation of the weather. Scientists in this scene are measuring air pressure with a barometer.

The weather has been studied for thousands of years. The Greek philosopher and scientist Aristotle published the first book about weather around 350 BC. Through the centuries, farmers and sailors observed changes in the wind, the clouds and the behavior of animals, but there were no accurate instruments to measure the weather. In the sixteenth century, however, Galileo invented the thermometer. In 1644, an Italian scientist called Torricelli invented the barometer, which measures atmospheric pressure. This was followed by the invention of the hygrometer, which measures humidity, and the anemometer, a device to measure wind speed. Soon, people were able to measure the effects of the weather, and forecasting became a more exact science. With the invention of the telegraph in 1837, it became possible to transmit weather information from remote weather stations to the rest of the world. Since then, forecasting has improved steadily.

DID YOU KNOW?
In the nineteenth century, the English used cameras and giant tripods to calculate the height of clouds. Meteorologists today use laser beams.

AN EARLY THERMOMETER
One of the earliest thermometers was a glass flask with a very long, thin tube standing in it. It was filled with alcohol and the end was sealed. The alcohol inside the tube expanded as the temperature outside increased, and contracted as the temperature cooled.

WEATHER VANE
Weather vanes have been used for thousands of years to show the direction of the wind. This gilt-bronze weather vane was crafted by Vikings in the tenth century.

A New Weather Bureau

In 1847, Joseph Henry, secretary of the Smithsonian Institution in the United States, established a system of meteorological observations. Telegraphic reports from weather stations all over the country were sent to the Institution. The information was analyzed each day. A large map was displayed at the Institution and a weather report sent to the *Washington Evening Post*. By 1869, more than 350 stations were sending in reports.

Measuring Weather

Y ou can get a rough idea of the weather that is on the way just by looking at the sky and checking the direction of the wind. But to find out what is really happening, you need to use accurate instruments to measure the different weather effects. Many of these instruments are simple and can be kept in the home. You can even keep daily weather records if you wish. The most important weather readings are temperature, rainfall, the speed and direction of the wind, air pressure and humidity. Readings should be taken at the same time each day. Sometimes the hours of sunlight and the amount of cloud cover are also noted. But taking the readings is only the first stage. Before the weather forecaster can predict the weather, he or she needs to put the readings together and compare them.

YOUR OWN WEATHER STATION
A simple weather station can be set up in a garden or school. A rain gauge, placed in the open, will collect rainwater and measure rainfall. These findings can be recorded and used to calculate average rainfall.

STRANGE BUT TRUE

In 1938, just before a hurricane hit Long Island, New York, a man received a new barometer through the mail. When the instrument read "hurricane" he thought the needle was stuck, so he wrote a letter of complaint to the manufacturers. When he returned from mailing the letter, he discovered that his home had been destroyed by a hurricane.

UNDER PRESSURE

Air pressure changes with the weather. Low pressure often means rain, or even a storm, while high pressure can mean settled or fair weather. A non-liquid barometer called an "aneroid" barometer measures the effect of air pressure on a box where the air has been removed. As the air pressure outside increases, the sides of the box are pushed in and the needle moves around the dial. If the air pressure falls, the sides of the box bulge out and the needle moves in the opposite direction around the dial.

ANEMOMETER

Anemometers measure wind speed. The faster the three cups spin, the higher the wind speed. Anemometers can be connected to computers for more accurate readings.

STORM GLASS

Because mercury barometers are expensive, water-filled storm glasses were commonly used on small boats in the nineteenth century. When the water rose up the spout of the glass, sailors knew that low pressure, a sign of stormy weather, was on the way.

STEVENSON SCREEN

A thermometer and hygrometer are usually kept inside a Stevenson screen, which shields them from direct sunlight.

Weather Watch

The Earth's atmosphere is a massive and constantly moving weather machine. Weather forecasters need to gather information about the atmosphere from all around the world, both at the Earth's surface and at heights of up to 2,480 miles (4,000 km). There are thousands of weather stations on land and at sea recording these changes in the atmosphere—the changes we call weather. These observations are backed up by balloons and aircraft that take atmospheric readings. In some places throughout the world, automatic and manual weather stations are found in remote places. All weather stations are required to take readings in the same way and their reports are gathered together for analysis by the World Meteorological Organization. Separate national organizations obtain the information necessary for preparing the forecasts we read or hear.

DID YOU KNOW?

Rain gauges were used in India as long ago as 400 BC. Farmers would place a number of small bowls in different places to catch rain. This helped them to learn about patterns of rainfall.

REMOTE READINGS

Meteorologists need information from all around the world, so there are weather stations in some extremely remote areas. Some stations are run by trained observers, although automatic weather stations are now becoming more common.

Weather balloon
Special balloons are released high into the atmosphere to obtain weather readings. Miniature radio transmitters, called radiosondes, are attached to the balloons. They broadcast information back to the ground.

Stevenson screen
Thermometers and hygrometers, which record temperature and humidity, are kept in here.

Campbell–Stokes recorder
This monitors the hours of sunlight in one day.

Low-level anemometer
This measures wind speed near the ground.

Evaporation pan
This instrument traps water and then records the rate at which it evaporates.

Rain gauge
This is placed in the open, to collect and measure rainfall over 24 hours.

Pluviograph
This automatically records the amount of rainfall on a chart.

SEA SPY

Conditions at sea are monitored by specially equipped ships and remote weather buoys. These buoys are towed to positions away from shipping lanes and anchored to the sea bed. It is important to watch the weather far out at sea, because severe storms and hurricanes form there.

EYE IN THE SKY

Meteorology, or the study of weather, changed dramatically in 1960, when the first weather satellites were launched into space. These satellites scan huge areas of the Earth and send back a range of measurements, as well as images of cloud cover and other weather conditions. This information enables meteorologists to plot the development and course of major events such as hurricanes, and predict the weather more accurately. By using satellite sensors that are sensitive to heat and light, meteorologists can also obtain information about the temperature of different types of clouds and the surface of the land and sea.

Meteorological satellite

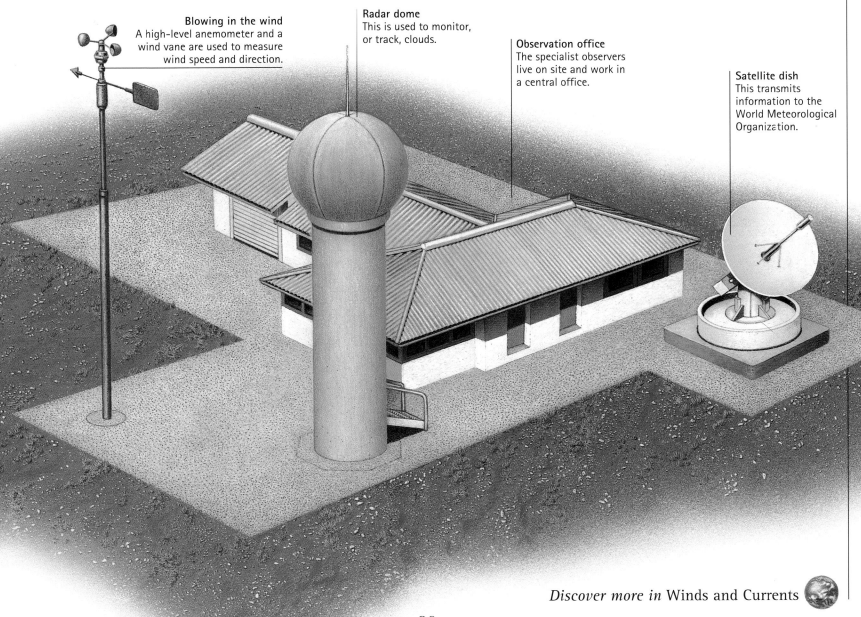

Blowing in the wind
A high-level anemometer and a wind vane are used to measure wind speed and direction.

Radar dome
This is used to monitor, or track, clouds.

Observation office
The specialist observers live on site and work in a central office.

Satellite dish
This transmits information to the World Meteorological Organization.

Discover more in Winds and Currents

Forecasting

Every minute of the day and night, weather recordings from observation stations, ships, planes and satellites are received by meteorological offices all around the world. These recordings form a vast databank, from which meteorologists gather information. The system that enables this huge exchange of information is the Global Telecommunications System (GTS). The data is fed into powerful computers that enable meteorologists to prepare weather maps known as synoptic charts. Meteorologists study these charts very carefully and compare them to previous charts before they produce a weather forecast. The weather presenters we see on television use synoptic charts to prepare weather maps with simple symbols such as rain clouds and yellow suns. Weather forecasts are 85 percent accurate for the next few days. However, it is far more difficult to predict the weather for more than a week ahead.

ON THE MAP
Synoptic charts contain a wealth of information including air pressure, wind speed and direction, cloud cover, temperature and humidity. The most noticeable features on the charts are isobars. These are lines that join places of equal air pressure and are measured in hectapascals. Isobars that are close together, as they are on this map, show an area of low pressure. This usually brings wind and rain.

ON THE DRAWING BOARD
Meteorologists spend many hours preparing synoptic charts. All the different information has to be carefully plotted on the chart.

KEY TO SYMBOLS

wind symbols		cloud symbols		weather symbols					
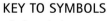	light		clear sky		cold front		snow		rain
	high		partly cloudy		warm front		fog		sleet
	gale force		cloudy	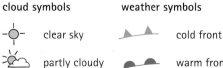	occluded front				

SUPER COMPUTING POWER

Supercomputers can carry out billions of calculations every second, and are essential for the accurate prediction of weather patterns. They are programmed to simulate, or imitate, the conditions of the weather using general circulation models. General circulation models try to predict what the world's weather will be like for short periods, such as the next few hours, and longer periods, such as the next ten years.

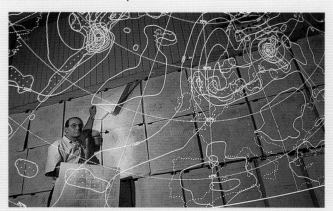

DID YOU KNOW?

The nineteenth-century Dutch meteorologist C.H.D. Buys Ballot was the first to use a system of shadings on a weather map to indicate areas of varying air pressure. He also made the discovery that wind flows from areas of high pressure to areas of low pressure.

Winds and Currents

Winds constantly circle the Earth. They bring rain and influence temperatures. The polar easterlies, prevailing westerlies and trade winds are called prevailing winds because they cover large sections of the Earth. Small, circular wind flows are called cells. Jet streams move air between these cells high in the atmosphere and at very high speeds. Sailors have known about the patterns of wind for centuries, and many of the winds, and areas near them, were named by early sailors. The horse latitudes, for example, occur in the Atlantic Ocean. When sailing ships with cargoes of horses for the New World encountered calm, hot weather in this area, many of the horses died. The Atlantic trade winds blew trading ships between Europe and the New World, while the narrow, windless area around the equator, called the doldrums, has frustrated sailors through time. Ocean currents follow the direction of the prevailing winds and affect both the climate of the world and our daily weather.

ON THE MOVE
These swirls in the ocean off the Norwegian coast are caused by currents and small whirlpools called eddies.

COMPUTER CURRENTS
Information about the oceans, including wind and temperature, are fed into computers that produce maps of ocean currents. This map shows an Antarctic current running across the bottom. The red areas indicate fast-flowing water while the blue areas are slow currents.

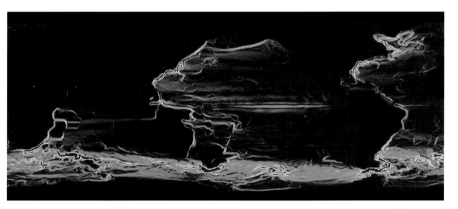

OCEAN CURRENTS

Ocean currents follow the direction of the prevailing winds. In each ocean there is a roughly circular movement of water called a gyre. Near the equator, the currents are blown toward the west, but at the poles the currents flow eastward. In this diagram it is possible to see the warm Gulf Stream. It runs up the coast of the eastern United States and then turns eastward across the Atlantic Ocean to Northern Europe. The Gulf Stream brings mild weather to parts of Northern Europe that would otherwise be much cooler.

→ warm currents → cool currents

Polar cell
Cold, dense air sinks and flows away from the poles and is replaced by warm air flowing in from above.

Polar jet stream
A band of air travels at high speed along the polar front.

Subtropical jet stream
A band of air travels at high speed.

Hadley cell
Warm air rises, moves away from the equator and sinks over the subtropics. Cool air flows toward the equator to replace it.

WINDS OF THE WORLD
The Earth spins as it orbits the sun. The winds do not blow in a straight line between high- and low-pressure areas, but are deflected. They bend to the right in the Northern Hemisphere and to the left in the Southern Hemisphere. This is called the Coriolis effect.

Ferrel cell
Warm, subtropical air flows toward the poles and cool, polar air flows toward the equator.

Doldrums
Low pressure area with light winds.

Trade winds
Dry winds blow from the northeast and southeast toward the equator, and replace rising, warm air.

Horse latitudes
A belt of high pressure is created when warm tropical air sinks to the ground. Winds blow out from this region.

FROM THE PAST
Knowledge of the direction of the winds around the world has improved over the last 2,000 years. This map drawn in AD 150 by Ptolemy, a Greek astronomer and geographer, shows the way many people saw the world until the sixteenth century.

Prevailing westerlies
Warm, moist winds blow toward the poles from the subtropics.

Polar easterlies
Cold winds blow from high-pressure regions over the poles.

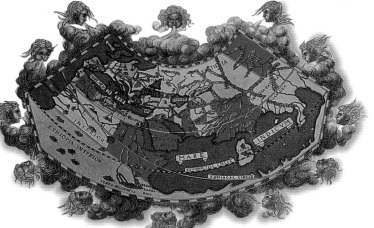

TOTAL CALM
In the past, sailing ships traveling across the equator were often becalmed in the doldrums. Sometimes they waited several weeks before the pattern of wind shifted and a breeze returned.

Discover more in The Weather Engine

43

World Climate

As the Earth is a sphere, the equator receives more heat from the sun's rays than the poles. Farther from the equator, the sun is weaker and less heat reaches the Earth's surface. The surface of the Earth is not heated equally, and this results in a pattern of winds moving the air around constantly. The intense heat of the equatorial sun causes warm, moisture-laden air to rise into the atmosphere. As this air cools, the moisture condenses and falls as rain. Warm air moves away from the equator and eventually sinks to the ground, which helps to form deserts such as the Sahara. Cool air is drawn back toward the equator to replace the rising, warm air. This sets up the circulations of air that produce the world's climates. The distribution of land and sea on the Earth, and the presence of mountain ranges, also affect climate. Coastal regions have milder climates than areas in the middle of a continent. Ocean currents influence climate as well. Northwest Europe has a mild climate because the warm waters of the Gulf Stream pass nearby.

WORLD CLIMATE REGIONS
This map shows the world's major climate zones. Climate is the typical weather of a region, based on average weather conditions over a period of at least 30 years.

THE SEASONS

Regular changes in weather patterns during the year are called seasons. In many parts of the world there are four seasons—spring, summer, fall and winter—while in other areas there are only two—a wet and a dry season. The Earth is tilted at an angle as it circles the sun. For six months of the year, the Northern Hemisphere is tilted toward the sun. It has long, warm, summer days while the Southern Hemisphere has short, cool winter days. For the next six months, the Northern Hemisphere is tilted away from the sun. This part of the world has winter while the Southern Hemisphere enjoys summer.

Solstice The sun appears to stop moving south on December 21. The Southern Hemisphere has its longest day, while the Northern Hemisphere has its shortest day.

Equinox On September 23, when the sun is over the equator, day and night are of equal length.

Solstice On June 21, the sun appears to stop moving north. Both hemispheres experience the reverse conditions of December 21.

Equinox On March 21, when the sun is over the equator, day and night are the same length.

44

POLAR ZONES

These are the coldest parts of the world. Winter temperatures fall below -58°F (-50°C).

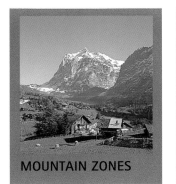

MOUNTAIN ZONES

These high altitudes have cold climates.

TEMPERATE ZONES

These have moderate temperature ranges.

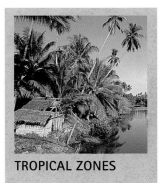

TROPICAL ZONES

These have average monthly temperatures of 80°F (27°C), and high rainfall.

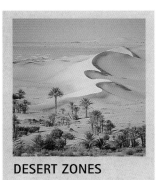

DESERT ZONES

Temperatures here may range from more than 104°F (40°C) in the day to freezing at night.

DID YOU KNOW?

The world's most extreme temperature range is in Verhoyansk, northeast Siberia. Temperatures there can fall to as low as -90°F (-68°C) in winter and rise to as high as 98°F (37°C) in summer.

Polar Zones

Climates near the North and South poles are characterized by freezing temperatures and permanent snow and ice. Polar summers are short and cold. The extreme climate is caused by lack of heat because the sun is weaker and the ice reflects much of the heat from the sun back into the atmosphere. For six months of the year, the Arctic experiences winter as the North Pole is tilted away from the sun. At the same time, Antarctica, the continent around the South Pole, enjoys a brief summer. Temperatures rise to freezing, or just above, near the coast. The pack ice drifts northward and melts in the warmer waters. Winter in the Antarctic, however, is severe. Antarctica doubles in size as the sea freezes over, and pack ice extends for hundreds of miles around the continent. Frequent blizzards and fierce winds rage across the icy surface.

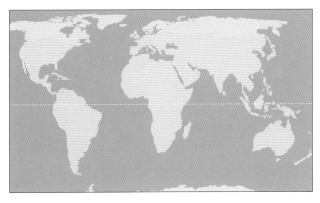

POLES APART
The Arctic is a frozen sea surrounding the North Pole, while the Antarctic is a frozen continent around the South Pole.

THE DEEP FREEZE
The Antarctic is covered in ice and snow, and the climate is bleak and hostile. Even in summer, temperatures barely reach freezing point. In spite of this, many animals live in the polar regions.

COAT OF COLORS

The fur of the Arctic fox changes color during the year. In winter, it turns from smoky gray to white to camouflage the fox against the snow.

ARCTIC DWELLERS

The Inuit (Eskimos), who live in the Arctic, have adapted well to the extreme climatic conditions.

WHITE OUT

Blizzards are strong winter snowstorms. They are particularly severe in the polar zones, where they may last for weeks at a time. Snow falls on more than 150 days of the year and is swept into huge piles by the wind. Winds are equally severe and reach speeds of more than 186 miles (300 km) per hour. The average winter temperatures plummet to -76°F (-60°C). In these extreme temperatures, unprotected human skin will freeze in seconds. People need layers of warm clothing and protective shelters to survive this bitter cold.

Nepal lies in the Himalayas. There is very little flat land for villages, so houses are scattered. The warm, sunny, south-facing slopes are used for farming. The north-facing slopes are usually forested. Because the steep slopes are difficult to farm, they have been gradually terraced to provide many small, level fields for farming. The higher pastures extend up to the permanent snow line.

CLINGING TO THE GROUND

The stems of alpine plants hug the ground to avoid the full force of the wind. Their leaves are small and waxy to reduce water loss. Because these plants grow only on warm days, they grow very slowly.

• CLIMATE •

Mountain Zones

Each mountain has its own weather pattern. Within a mountain range there may be varying climatic conditions—the side of a mountain facing the wind may experience higher precipitation than the more sheltered side. Even the position of a rock or tree, creating a barrier to the wind or snow, can have an effect on the climatic conditions. The air temperature decreases by a few degrees for every few hundred yards rise in altitude. The air becomes thinner, the sky bluer and the sun's rays stronger. On the highest mountains, there is snow and ice all year round. Nothing can survive permanently on mountain peaks that are more than 23,000 ft (7,000 m) high, because fierce winds and low temperatures would freeze any living cells. Mountain weather is very changeable too. It can be bright and sunny, then stormy. Warm daytime temperatures may be followed by bitterly cold nights.

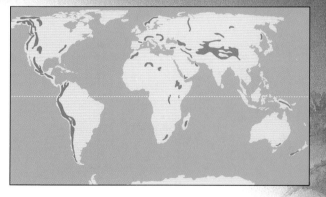

MOUNTAIN SITES
The areas highlighted above show the mountain zones around the world.

A SURE FOOTING
Mountain goats are nimble animals that can leap from rock to rock. They are found on the highest slopes, where they are safe from predators.

48

FLYING HIGH
Strong, gusty mountain winds make flying difficult for all but the largest birds. Eagles have broad wings that are ideal for gliding. They make good use of rising air currents to soar around the mountain peaks.

SNOW FUN

Over the last 100 years, skiing has become a popular winter sport in the mountains of Europe, North America, New Zealand, Asia and Australia. The snow-covered high mountains are used as ski runs, and ski lifts carry skiers from the valleys to the slopes. But alpine environments are slowly being damaged by all the activity in these mountain areas.

SEASONAL CHANGES

Temperate regions have distinct seasons. In spring, plants begin to produce leaves and flowers and animals start to breed. This period of growth peaks in summer. As fall approaches, deciduous trees begin to drop their leaves and many animals migrate, while others prepare to hibernate. During the winter months, snow may cover the ground for weeks at a time, and the barren landscape shows little sign of activity.

• CLIMATE •

Temperate Zones

The temperate zones of the world experience a mild, moist climate dominated by cool, moist air blowing from the poles toward the tropical zones. Large swings in temperature, the distance from the equator and the varying hours of sunlight create a changeable climate with distinct seasons. The temperate zones can be divided into three regions: warm temperate between 35 and 45 degrees latitude; cool temperate between 45 and 60 degrees latitude; and cold temperate, which is experienced by regions lying in the center of continents. The majority of people live in the temperate zones, where there is an adequate supply of water for most of the year. The world's temperate grasslands are found in these zones, where huge herds of grazing animals such as buffalo once roamed. Today, farmers keep sheep and cattle, and much of the grassland has been plowed to grow crops and grains.

AROUND THE WORLD
The temperate zones lie between 35 and 60 degrees latitude, north and south of the equator.

A CHANGE OF COLOR
Many trees have adapted to the temperate seasons. They lose their leaves during the cold months and create spectacular fall scenes such as this.

BUSY BEES

Honey bees need warmth to maintain a regular body temperature. They have adapted to the conditions in temperate zones to keep up their busy way of life.

TEMPERATE CITIES

There are differences between warm-temperate and cool-temperate climates. The warm-temperate areas receive most of their rainfall in winter and have hot, dry summers. The lack of water in summer means that the vegetation is sparse and shrubby. Cool-temperate areas have cold winters with heavy snowfall and warm, humid summers. Because rain falls all year round, vegetation is plentiful.

Winter in a warm-temperate climate

Winter in a cool-temperate climate

DID YOU KNOW?

The world's climate is constantly changing. Between the fifteenth and nineteenth centuries, the River Thames in London, England froze over every year. But this has not happened for the last 160 years.

Discover more in Temperature and Humidity

51

Tropical Zones

Tropical zones are the warmest regions of the world. The sun is overhead for most of the year, so the climate is always hot. But there are many variations of climate within the tropical zones. Tropical wet climates are hot and humid all through the year, and have very heavy rainfall. These regions lie close to the equator and have dense tropical rainforests. Hot air, laden with moisture, rises into the atmosphere during the day. As the air cools, the water condenses to form dark clouds that bring heavy rain in the afternoons. In a tropical dry climate, a wet season is usually followed by a dry one. The wet season has heavy rain storms and hot, humid weather. The temperature can be even higher in the dry season as the days are sunny and clear. The subtropics are regions that border the tropics, and they are mostly dry.

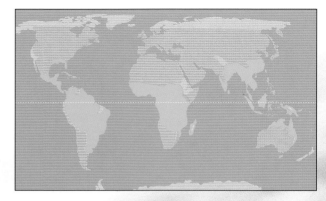

TROPICAL AND SUBTROPICAL SITES
Tropical zones lie between 30 degrees latitude north and south of the equator. Subtropical zones border these zones.

IN THE WET
When a low-pressure area develops over the land, cool, moist air from the ocean flows in. The air warms and rises as it crosses the land, and forms widespread rain clouds. The rains brought by these winds are called monsoons, and they provide 85 percent of Asia's annual rainfall.

TROPICAL DIVERSITY
In areas of South America, high temperatures and heavy rainfall support the lushest vegetation found on Earth: tropical rainforests. Many species of animal live in rainforests and feed on the fast-growing plants.

A DRY TIME
A high-pressure area over the land causes the winds to change direction. It rains out at sea and the land becomes dry.

THE SUBTROPICS

The subtropics lie to the north and south of the tropical zones. These areas do not receive as much rain as the tropics, but the temperature can be much higher. During the dry season, hot, scorching winds blow off the deserts. The ground dries and the vegetation becomes parched. As the sun moves overhead, the dry winds are replaced by hot, humid winds carrying moisture. This marks the beginning of the rainy season, which may last for several months. Zimbabwe (below) lies in a subtropical area.

Desert Zones

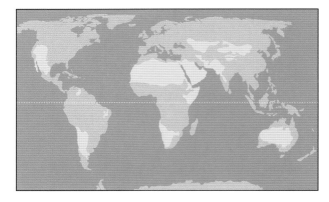

Deserts cover one-seventh of the Earth's land surface. They are dry regions that on average receive less than 4 in (100 mm) of rain per year. In some deserts, rain may not fall for many years. Then, quite suddenly, a storm will break and there is a huge downpour that lasts just a few hours. The absence of moisture in the air means that clouds are rare and the skies are clear for most of the year. The land is heated by the sun and daytime temperatures soar to 104°F (40°C) and above. However, the lack of cloud cover means that much of the heat radiates back into the atmosphere at night, and the air temperature plummets to almost freezing. Although they are dry and often very windy, not all deserts are hot. The cold winds that blow across the Gobi desert of central Asia produce freezing conditions, but it is still considered a desert because it has very little rain.

DESERT SITES
Deserts are found in subtropical areas, on the dry side of mountain ranges and in the center of large continents.

OVER THE DUNES
The strong winds in sandy deserts often create vast areas of sand dunes. The constantly shifting sand and the lack of water mean that there are few plants. Nomadic peoples often use camels as pack animals because they can survive with little water.

THE DESERT IN BLOOM

Every year, desert rains trigger the germination of thousands of plants. They grow rapidly so that they can complete their life cycle before they run out of water. A few weeks after rain has fallen, the desert is transformed into a carpet of flowers. These soon die, but their seeds lie in the ground, waiting for the next rainfall.

CREATURES OF THE DESERT

Lizards are well adapted to living in the desert. Their scaly skin enables them to retain water by cutting down evaporation. They also produce solid waste rather than liquid urine, and they can alter the color of their skin to reflect more or less heat. Desert animals have also adapted to survive. The large ears of the fennec fox enable it to lose heat from its body. The fox also has exceptional hearing and this allows it to hunt at night when temperatures are cooler. After the rains, honey pot ants collect as much nectar as they can find and give it to special ants that store the nectar in their abdomens. The ants' abdomens swell up, often to the size of grapes. During the dry months, the other ants in the colony feed off this collected honey.

Fennec fox

Honey pot ants

Q: Why do plants grow rapidly in the desert?

55

TREE RINGS

Each year, a tree grows a ring of woody material that is called an "annual ring." In warm, wet years, growth is good and the ring is wide. During years of bad weather, the ring is very narrow.

PAST ICE AGES

In the last million years, there have been four ice ages. The average temperature of the Earth during these times was 6–8 degrees below today's averages.

UNDER ICE

About two million years ago, the Earth's climate cooled and the polar ice cap expanded to cover northern Europe.

A MAMMOTH EVENT

Until the Würm Ice Age, huge, elephant-like mammoths lived on the cold plains that now form Siberia. The mammoths and other giant mammals disappeared as the climate became warmer and the ice retreated. Because the ice preserved their bodies, we know that they had thick, woolly coats and huge tusks.

CARVED BY ICE

A glacier is a mass of ice that flows very slowly down a mountain valley. It rubs away the sides of the valley until the valley becomes a U shape.

• CLIMATIC CHANGE •

Global Freezing

The Earth's climate has changed many times in the last few million years. There were periods of severe cold, known as ice ages or glacials, when great slabs of ice inched across the land. They gouged out hollows in their path as they pushed soil and rocks ahead of them. The sea level dropped enormously as much of the water froze. Warmer times between the ice ages were called interglacials. The ice melted and the huge hollows filled with water and became lakes. Scientists learn about the different climates in the Earth's history by looking for clues in nature. Some trees have lived for thousands of years and show signs of climatic changes. Fossils also provide valuable clues about wildlife and their environment. Most evidence about past climates comes by studying sediment samples from the beds of the oceans or ice samples taken from Greenland or Antarctica.

HIDDEN CLUES

Geologists can break open rocks to find the fossilized imprint of plants millions of years after the sediment originally built up.

THE LITTLE ICE AGE

Between 1430 and 1850, northern Europe experienced a "little ice age." It was not as severe as a full ice age, but the climate became colder, crops failed and there was widespread starvation. England experienced some of the coldest winters on record during the 1810s and 1820s. The River Thames froze over regularly and Frost Fairs, where people played games and danced, were held on its icy surface. Sometimes the weather warmed without warning. People had to flee quickly as the ice beneath them began to thaw and crack.

Discover more in Polar Zones

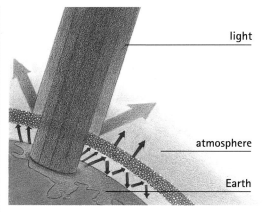

THE GREENHOUSE EFFECT

light

atmosphere

Earth

The Earth's atmosphere is like a greenhouse. It allows light from the sun to pass through it and heat the Earth's surface. Gases in the atmosphere, such as carbon dioxide, absorb the returning heat and also warm the surface. Without this greenhouse effect, the Earth would be too cold for life. But the level of carbon dioxide and other gases in the atmosphere is increasing. As more heat is absorbed by the atmosphere, the Earth becomes warmer and warmer.

• CLIMATIC CHANGE •

Global Warming

The Earth is getting warmer. Most of the hottest years during the twentieth century have occurred in the last decade. Scientists are still arguing whether this is due to the greenhouse effect or some other cause. One of the key factors in the greenhouse effect is carbon dioxide. This greenhouse gas traps heat in the Earth's atmosphere. Each year, more than 5,500 billion tons (5,100 billion tonnes) of carbon dioxide are absorbed by green plants to make food in a process called photosynthesis. This process produces oxygen, which living organisms need to breathe. However, the level of carbon dioxide in the atmosphere is increasing dramatically because of pollution, deforestation, farming methods and the burning of more fossil fuels (coal, gas and oil). Some scientists believe that the Earth's temperature will continue to rise as more carbon dioxide is released into the atmosphere.

A CHANGING WORLD

More fossil fuels are being used each year. They provide power for cars and industry, and heat homes and offices. When fossil fuels are burned, carbon dioxide is released. Cows also have a major effect on the atmosphere because they produce methane gas when they digest grass. As the number of cows increases, so does the amount of methane released.

POTENT METHANE

The greenhouse gas methane is 20 times stronger than carbon dioxide. Much of it comes from bacteria that live in waterlogged soils, such as rice paddy fields and wetlands.

A HOLE IN THE SKY

The ozone layer, which is in the upper atmosphere, shields the surface of the Earth from ultraviolet light. But scientists have discovered that the ozone layer is being attacked by manufactured chemicals called chlorofluorocarbons (CFCs), which are used in spray cans, refrigeration and air-conditioning. The blue at the center of this picture shows a hole in the ozone layer over Antarctica. This allows more ultraviolet light to reach Australia and New Zealand. In 1987, many nations around the world signed a treaty to limit the production of CFCs. This has been effective, but the damaging effects of CFCs will last for decades.

DISAPPEARING FORESTS
Trees absorb carbon dioxide and release oxygen. But forests are being cleared throughout the world. This deforestation is contributing to the increased levels of carbon dioxide in the atmosphere.

NEW LIFE
Replanting trees (reforestation) helps to reduce the greenhouse effect and fight global warming.

Discover more in Weather Watch

In the Extremes

RECORD WIND
On April 12, 1934, winds of 230 miles (371 km) per hour—the fastest surface winds ever recorded—swept across Mount Washington in New Hampshire.

TWISTING ON
A tornado that tore through Illinois and Indiana on May 26, 1917 left a track of 292 miles (471 km)—the longest ever seen.

THE HEAT IS ON
The highest temperature in the world, 136.4°F (58°C), was recorded at Al Aziziyah in Libya on September 13, 1922.

HERE COMES THE RAIN
Rain falls on Mount Wai'ale'ale in Hawaii on 350 days of the year. This creates an extraordinary average rainfall of 486 in (12,346 mm) each year.

SNOWED UNDER

Between April 14 and 15, 1921, at least 75 in (193 cm) of snow fell on Silver Lake in Colorado. This was the greatest snowfall in a 24-hour period.

ICE FROM ABOVE

The largest single hailstone to fall to the ground was recorded at Coffeyville, Kansas, on September 3, 1970. It weighed 1.67 lb (750 g) and had a diameter of 17½ inches (44 cm).

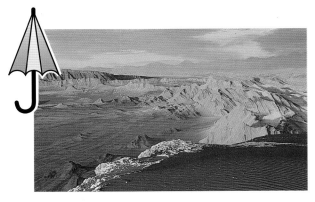

DRY AS A BONE
The driest place in the world, with an average annual rainfall of less than 1/250 in (0.1 mm) is the Atacama Desert in Chile.

RUMBLING CLOUDS
Bogor on the island of Java, Indonesia, can experience thunder on as many as 322 days each year.

HIGH PRESSURE
The highest ever barometric pressure, 1083.8 hectapascals, was recorded on December 31, 1968 in Siberia.

HERE COMES THE SUN
At the eastern end of the Sahara Desert in North Africa, the sun shines 97 percent of the possible daylight hours.

LOW PRESSURE
The lowest ever barometric pressure, 877 hectapascals, was recorded to the north of Guam in the Pacific Ocean in 1958.

DOWN THE SPOUT
On May 16, 1898, a waterspout with a height of 5,012 ft (1,528 m) and a diameter of 10 ft (3 m) was spotted off the coast of New South Wales, Australia.

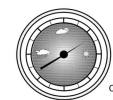

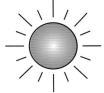

COLD AS ICE
The coldest place in the world is Vostok Base in Antarctica. It has an annual average temperature of −72°F (−58.2°C). On July 21, 1983, it recorded the world's lowest temperature, −128.6°F (−89.2°C).

61

Glossary

Radiosonde

Seasons

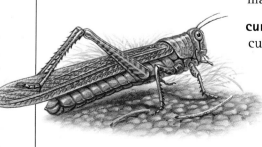

Rainbow

Grasshopper

altocumulus Puffy, white clouds at mid-altitude.

altostratus A layer of clouds at mid-altitude.

anemometer An instrument that measures wind direction and speed.

anticyclone A system of rotating winds spiralling out from a high pressure area. Generally associated with stable weather.

atmosphere The thin layer of gases that envelops the Earth.

atmospheric pressure The force exerted by air on its surroundings.

barometer An instrument for measuring atmospheric pressure.

blizzard A snowstorm with strong winds.

chlorofluorocarbons (CFCs) Synthetic substances used in aerosol sprays, refrigeration, foam plastics and fire extinguishers.

cirrocumulus High altitude, fluffy clouds.

cirrostratus A layer of high-altitude clouds.

cirrus High altitude, wispy clouds made of ice crystals.

climate The average weather conditions in a particular region over a period of at least 30 years.

cloud A visible mass of water droplets and ice floating in the air, formed when water condenses.

condensation When water changes from a vapor to a liquid.

convection The upward movement of a mass of warm air, rising through cooler, denser air.

Coriolis effect The deflection of winds caused by the spinning of the Earth.

crystal A solid substance made up of atoms, molecules or ions, for example, an ice crystal made of frozen water.

cumulonimbus A towering, dark mass of cumulus clouds associated with thunder and lightning.

cumulus Fluffy, low-altitude clouds.

current A flow of water or air.

cyclone A violent tropical storm, also known as a hurricane or a typhoon.

deciduous A term used to describe plants that drop their leaves in fall.

deforestation Widespread clearing of a forest.

depression A low-pressure region often associated with rain.

desert An area that receives little rain.

drizzle Light rain, with water drops less than $1/5$ in (0.5 mm) in diameter.

drought A prolonged period without any rain.

equator An imaginary line that lies halfway between the North and South poles.

equinox Either of the two occasions, six months apart, when day and night are of equal length.

evaporation A change in state from a liquid to a gas.

fog A dense, low cloud of water droplets lying near to the ground, which reduces visibility to less than 3,608 ft (1,100 m).

fossil The remains or imprint of a plant or animal found in rock.

frost An icy coating that forms when moisture in the air freezes.

glacier A slow-moving mass of ice, formed in mountains, which creeps down valleys.

global warming The gradual increase in the average global temperature from year to year.

greenhouse effect The trapping of heat energy by certain gases in the atmosphere.

gyre The circular movement of water in an ocean.

hail Hard, icy pellets formed in cumulonimbus clouds, which are solid when they reach the ground.

hibernation When an animal goes into a deep sleep with reduced body temperature and heart rate in order to survive a cold winter.

humidity The amount of water vapor in the air.

hurricane A large tropical depression with high winds and torrential rainfall. Also called a cyclone or a typhoon.

hygrometer An instrument that measures the amount of moisture in the air.

ice age A cold period during which ice extends over as much as one-third of the Earth's surface.

insulation A layer of material that reduces the loss of heat from a body or a building.

interglacial A warm period with tropical conditions found over much of the land surface.

isobar A line on a map joining points of equal atmospheric pressure.

latitudes Imaginary lines drawn around the Earth parallel to the equator. Imaginary lines from one pole to the other are called longitudes.

lightning A flash of electricity in the sky usually generated during a thunderstorm.

meteorologist A person who studies the weather.

meteorology The study of the weather.

monsoon A wind that changes direction, bringing heavy rain during the wet season.

nimbostratus A low-level, dark cloud that produces rain.

ozone A colorless gas made up of three oxygen atoms.

ozone layer A diffuse layer of ozone molecules found high in the atmosphere. It filters out harmful ultraviolet radiation from the sun.

pack ice Ice that forms when the surface of the ocean freezes.

photosynthesis The process in which plants make their own food using carbon dioxide, water and light.

precipitation Water or ice, such as snow, sleet or rain, which falls to the ground from clouds.

radiosonde A device attached to a weather balloon released into the high atmosphere to monitor weather conditions.

rainfall The amount of rain received by a particular region over a set period.

reflection When light bounces off a surface.

refraction The bending of light as it passes from one substance into another.

season A weather period of the year.

sleet A mixture of snow and rain.

smog A fog contaminated with air pollutants, which react together in the presence of sunlight.

snow Falling ice crystals.

solstice Either the shortest day of the year (winter solstice) or the longest day of the year (summer solstice).

spectrum The rainbow colors that white light produces when it passes through a water droplet or a glass prism.

stratocumulus A layer of fluffy clouds at low altitude.

stratus A layer of low, gray clouds covering the sky.

sweating The evaporation of liquid from the surface of the skin, which cools the body.

synoptic chart A weather map showing conditions at a particular point in time.

temperate Moderate or mild conditions.

temperature A measure of the amount of heat.

thermometer An instrument that measures the temperature.

thunder A rumbling shock wave created when lightning heats the air.

tornado A violent, spiraling wind that is short-lived but destructive.

tropical Hot and often humid conditions experienced in regions close to the equator.

typhoon A violent tropical storm, also known as a hurricane or a cyclone.

vapor A gaslike state of a solid or liquid.

waterspout A tornado at sea.

weather The atmospheric conditions experienced at a particular place or time.

weather satellite An orbiting instrument that monitors atmospheric conditions and transmits the information back to Earth.

wind A mass of air that moves from one place to another.

Dragonfly

Formation of a rainbow

Hygrometer

Measuring the weather

Index

Picture Credits

(t=top, b=bottom, l=left, r=right, c=center, F=front, C=cover,
B=back, Bg=background)
AIATSIS, 33bl (Museum of Australia). Ancient Art & Architecture
Collection, 4tl, 32c. Ann Ronan Picture Library, 29br. Art Resource, 35bl.
Auscape, 14br (G. Boutin/Explorer), 55tl (J.M. La Roque), 48br (M. Newman).
Austral International, 9cr (FPG International). Australian Geographic, 3,
37cl, 37tl. Australian Picture Library, 9bcr (R. Bisson), 7tl, 17bl, 45tl
(J. Carnemolla), 25br, 49tr (ZEFA). Johnny C. Autery, 23c. Bilderberg,
41tr (P. Ginter). Bruce Coleman Limited, 56c (E. Pott), 45tcr (A. Price),
24bl (H. Reinhard), 47tl (J. Shaw), 28bl (U. Walz). Bryan and Cherry
Alexander, 46tl, 47c, 47tr. Burke Museum, 32br (E. Calderon). Christine
Osborne Pictures, 45tr (C. Barton). Densey Clyne, 55c. Earth Images, 26tl
(T. Domico), 20c (A. Ruid). Ecoscene, 48cl (Chelmick). Frank Lane Picture
Archive, 25tr (J.C. Allen), 22b (R. Jennings). Michael Freeman, 61tr.
The Granger Collection, 11tl, 17tl, 57b. Hedgehog House, 61br (D. Smith).
Horizon Photo Library, 7tr (H. Ecker), 51tl, 59tr. The Image Bank, 52tl
(J.H. Carmichael), 45tc (H.G. Ross/Stockphotos, Inc), 7cl (S. Wilkinson).
International Photographic Library, 31c (SuperStock), 11tr, 31tl, 58bl.
International Stock, 12tc (W. Faidley), 22tr (B. Firth), 26c (M.P. Manheim).
J. Allan Cash Ltd, 27tr, 28tl. Richard Keen, 27cr. Bob Litchfield, 51tr.
Lochman Transparencies, 21br (B. Downs). Mary Evans Picture Library,

43br. Minden Pictures, 59cr (F. Lanting). National Meteorological Library,
39tl (Crown), 28tr (F. Gibson). The Nature Company, 37tc. Paul Nevin, 40cl.
North Wind Picture Archives, 43bl. Oxford Scientific Films, 20bc (D. Allan),
55tr (E. Bartov), 49tl (B. Bennett). Pacific Stock, 60bl (M. Van Deven). Peter
Arnold Inc, 60tl (C.H. Smith). The Photo Library, Sydney, 6cr (K. Biggs/TSW),
6bl (F. Grant), 61tl (N. Green), 42c (Los Alamos National Laboratory/SPL),
6/7b (SPL), 9br (SPL/NASA). Photo Researchers, Inc, 12tr (L.J. Georgia),
13cr (Hasler & Pierce, NASA, GSFC/Science Source), 16br (D. McIntyre).
Photri, 39tr. Planet Earth Pictures, 21c (J.R. Bracegirdle), 50br
(J. Eastcott/YVA Momatiuk), 56br (K. Lucas), 10tl, 59br (J. Lythgoe), 42tr
(R. Matthews), 46/47c (K. Puttock). Robert Harding Picture Library, 7cr
(M. Jenner), 53tl (Raleigh International), 7br, 14bl, 51tcr, 56cr. Scala, 4r,
34l. South American Pictures, 33bc (T. Morrison). Stock Photos, 45tcl
(H.P. Merten/TSM), 6tr (G. Monro), 19bl (R. Richardson), 18br
(J. Towers/TSM). Werner Forman Archive, 32bl (Private Collection),
34br (Statens Historiska Museum, Stockholm).

56/57t, 57r. Nick Farmer/Brihton Illustration, 11-14c, 11c, 13bc.
Rod Ferring, 28/29c, 28cr, 63tcr. Mike Gorman, 24/25c, 38/39b, 40/41c,
62tl. Lorraine Hannay, 4bl, 36/37b, 36l, 37r, 63br. Tim Harrison, 60/61c.
Richard Hook/Bernard Thornton Artists, UK, 34/35t, 35r. Roger Kent/
Garden Studio, 26/27c. Jillian B. Luff, 12tl, 42b, 46tr, 48cr, 50cr, 52tr,
54tr, 56c. Iain McKellar, 2, 16l, 16c, 17r, 17c, 63cr. Tony Pyrzakowski,
32/33t, 33r. Oliver Rennert, 5t, 8/9c, 8tl, 10/11c, 10bl, 10tr, 18/19c,
19tl, 19tr, 43c, 44bc, 62cl. Trevor Ruth, 48/49c, 54/55c. Michael
Saunders, 52/53b. Stephen Seymour/Bernard Thornton Artists, UK,
58/59c, 58tl. Ray Sim, 22c, 22cl, 22cr, 22tl, 23cr. Rod Westblade, 1,
20l, 52bl, 52cl, 62bcl, endpapers, icons. Melissa Wilton, 60/61 map
key symbols.

Cover Credits

Ad-Libitum, Bg (S. Bowey). Ray Grinaway, FCtl, FCtr. Iain McKellar,
BCtl. Photri, BCbr. Fred K. Smith, FCc.

Illustration Credits

Mike Atkinson/Garden Studio, 5tr, 30b, 30l, 31r, 31b, 62bl, 63tr.
Kenn Backhaus, 44/45c. Andrew Beckett/Garden Studio, 5br, 50/51c,

Acknowledgments

Special thanks to the Bureau of Meteorology, Australia.